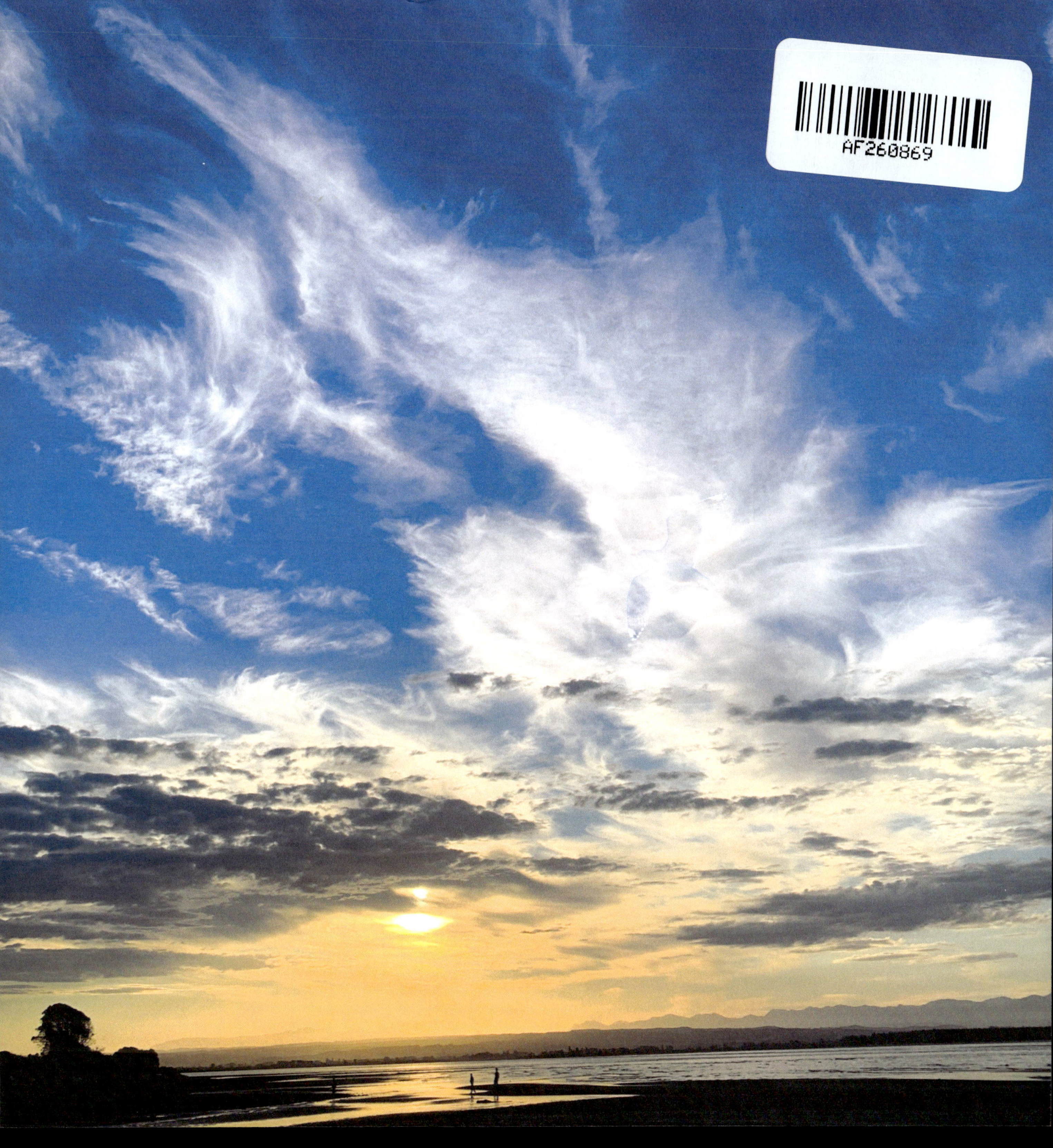

AF260869

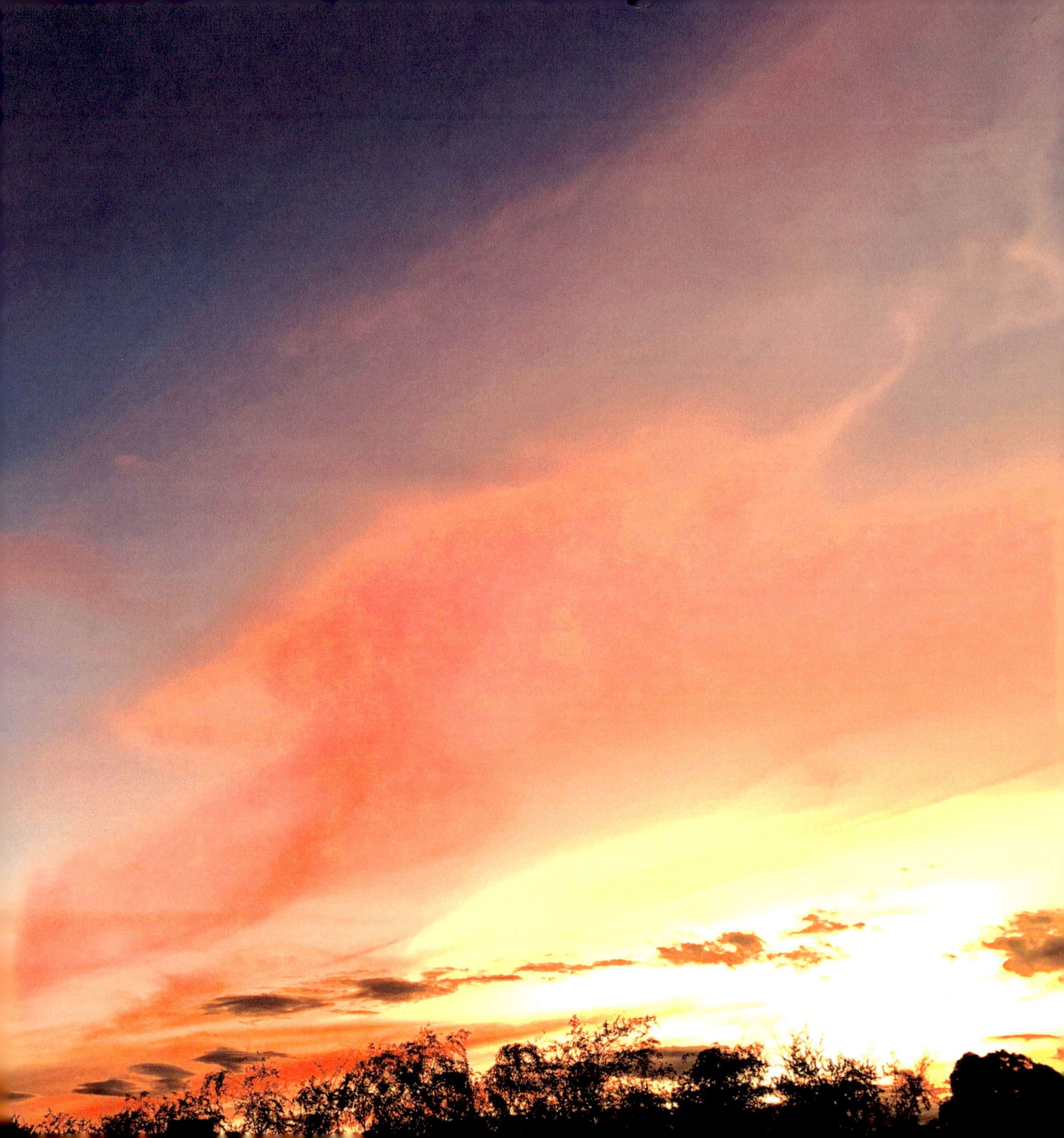

Heavenward Prayers

Scripture Art

Your name:

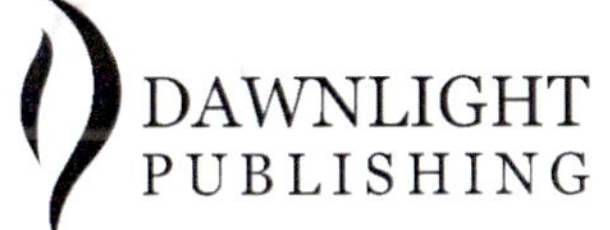

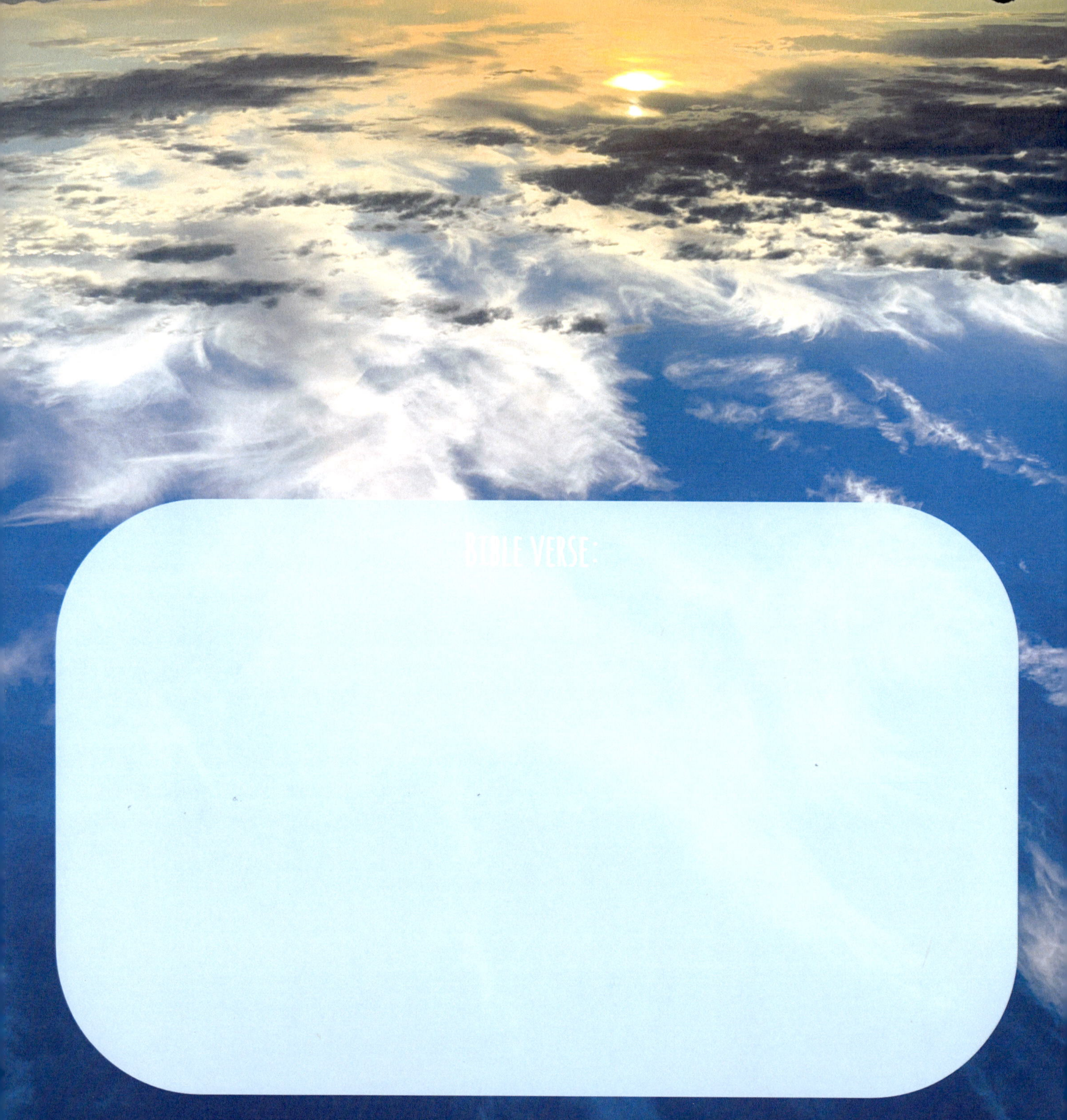

BIBLE VERSE:

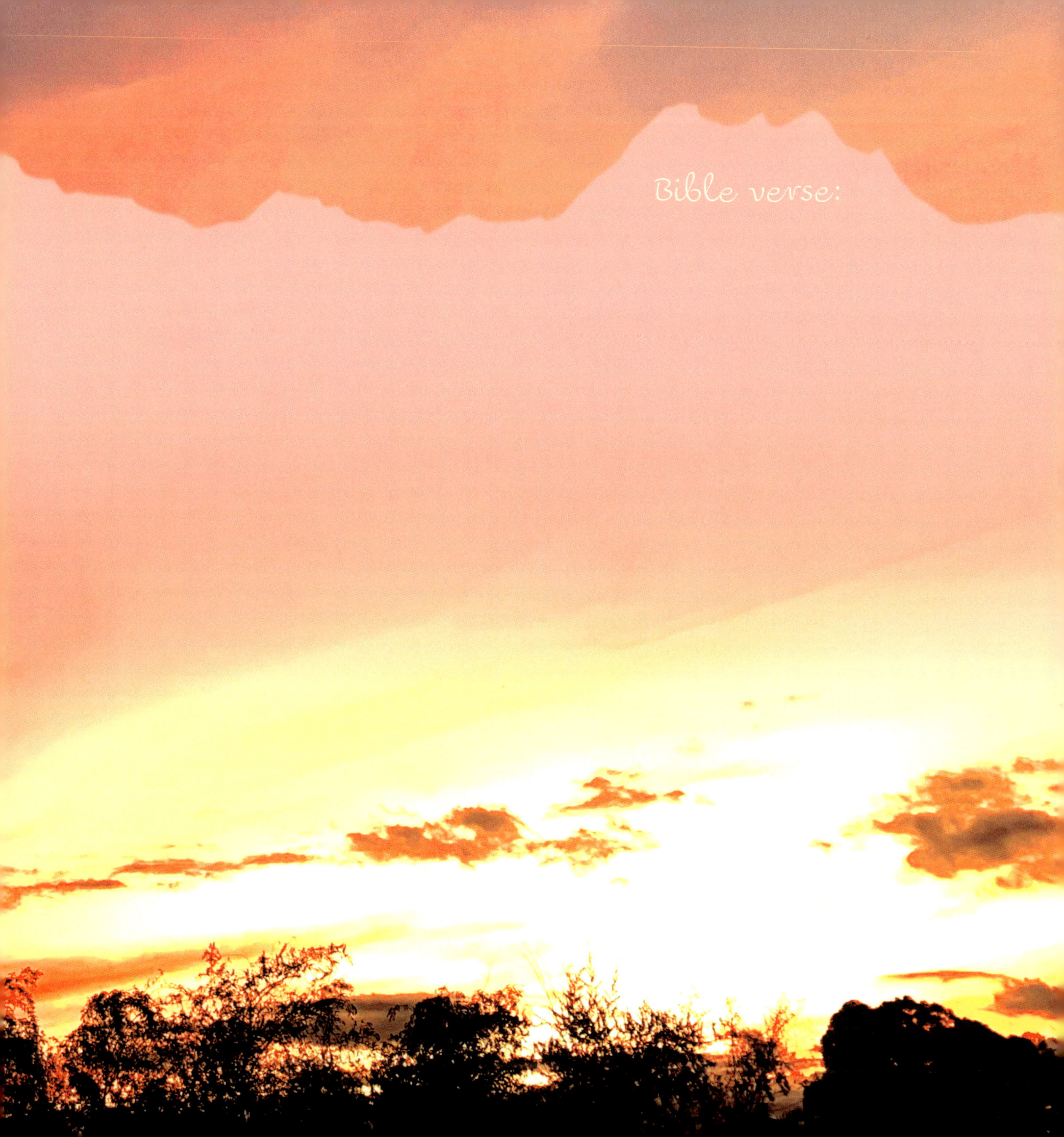
Bible verse:

Personal prayer:

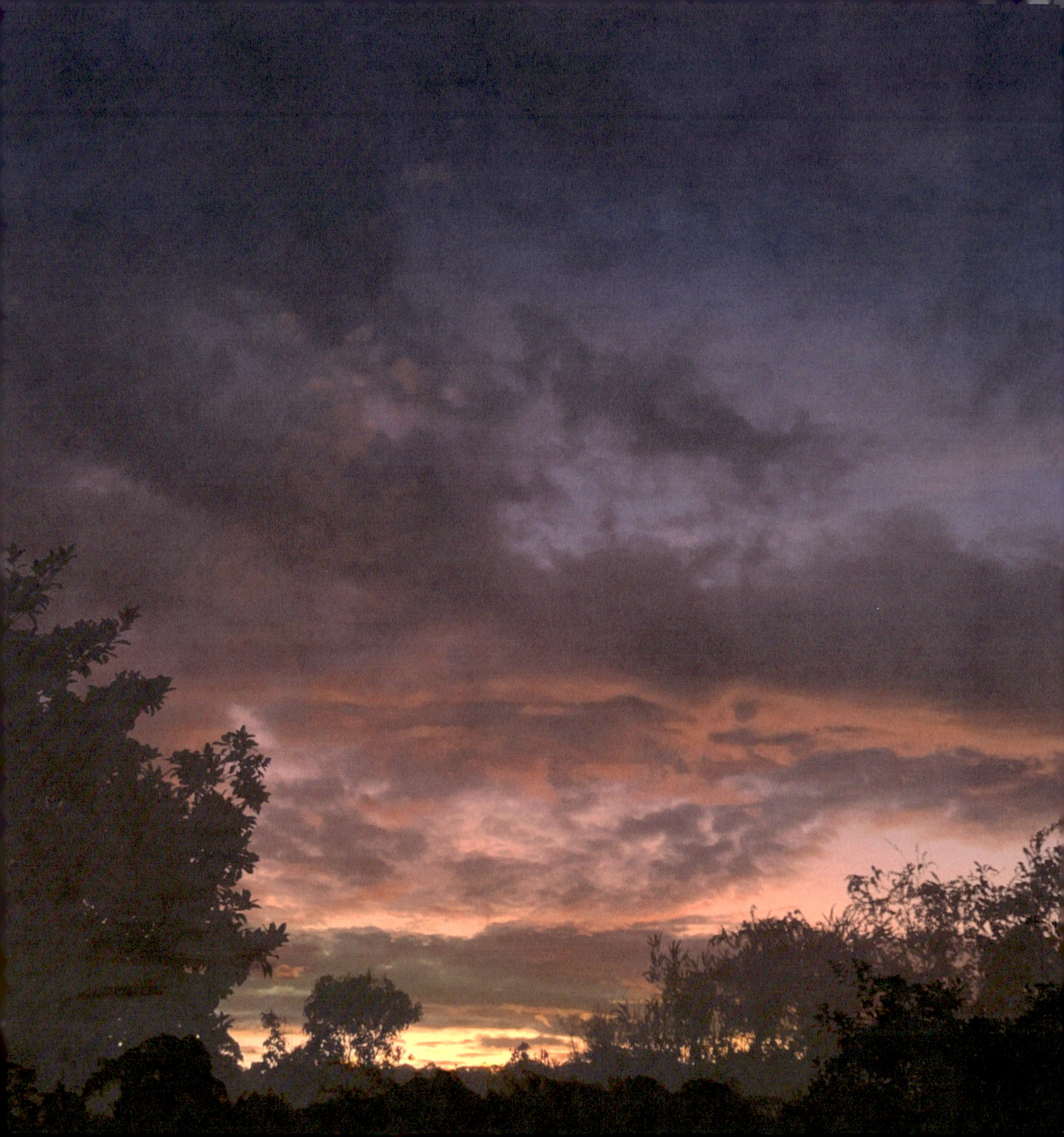

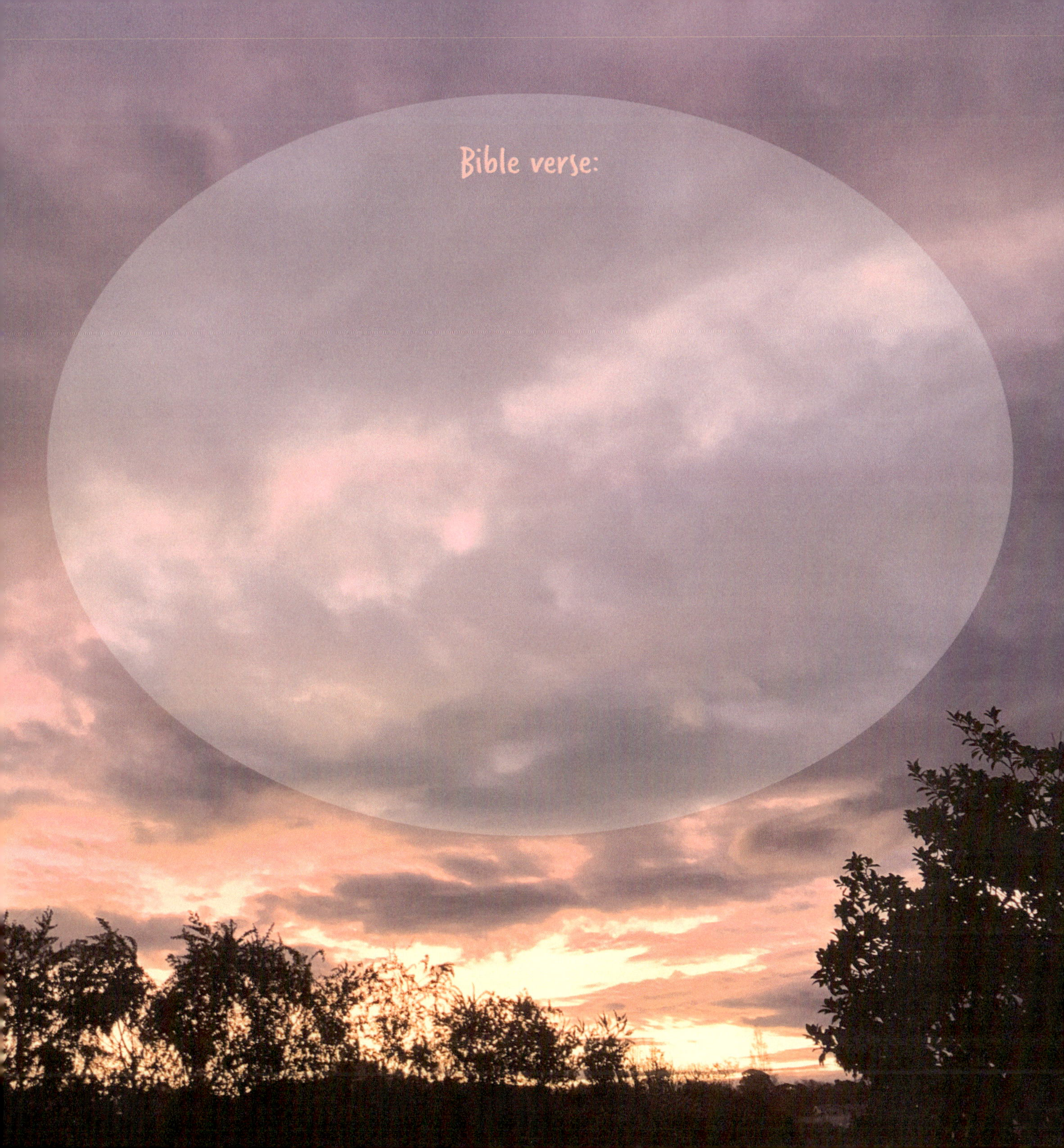

Bible verse:

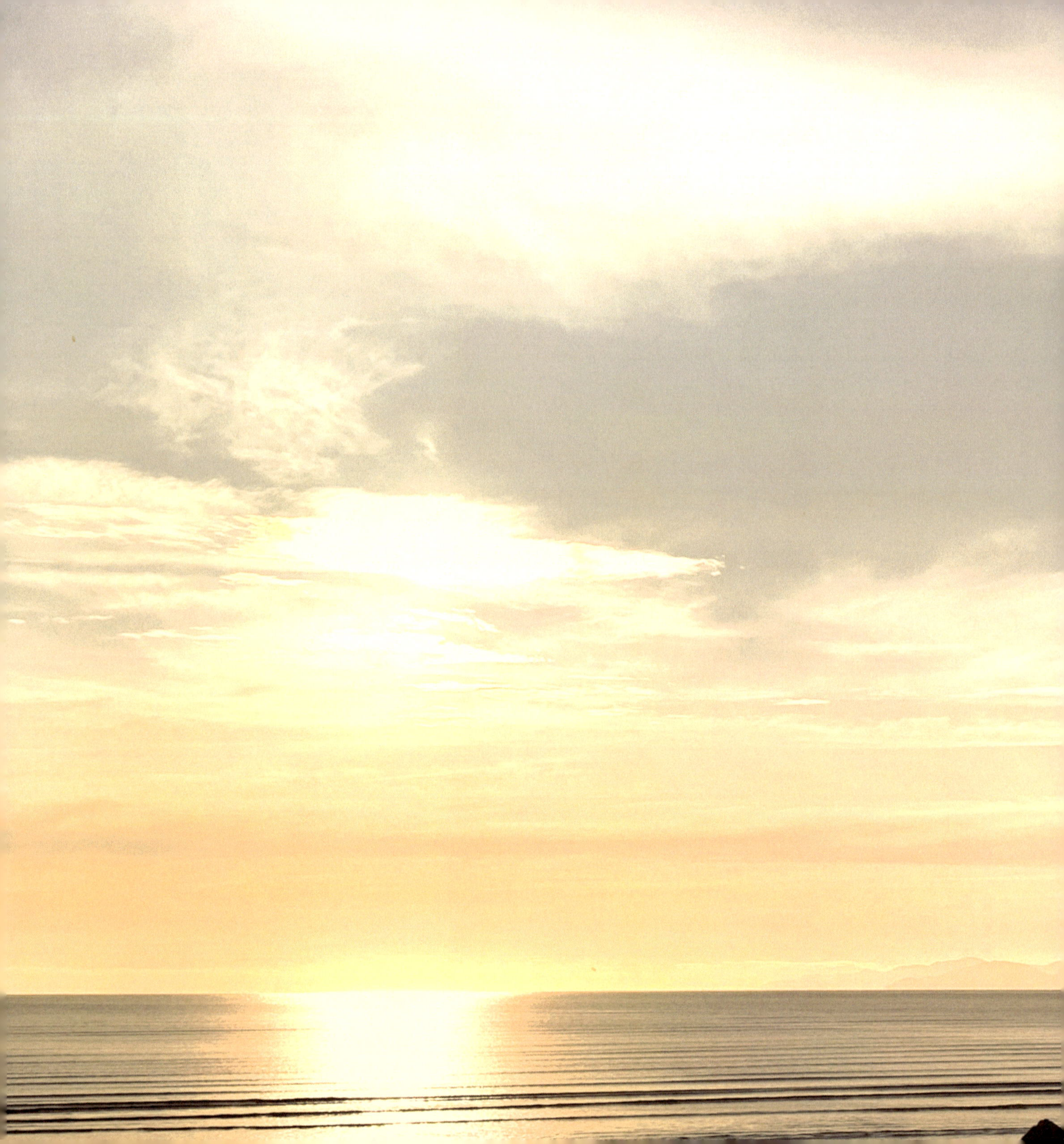

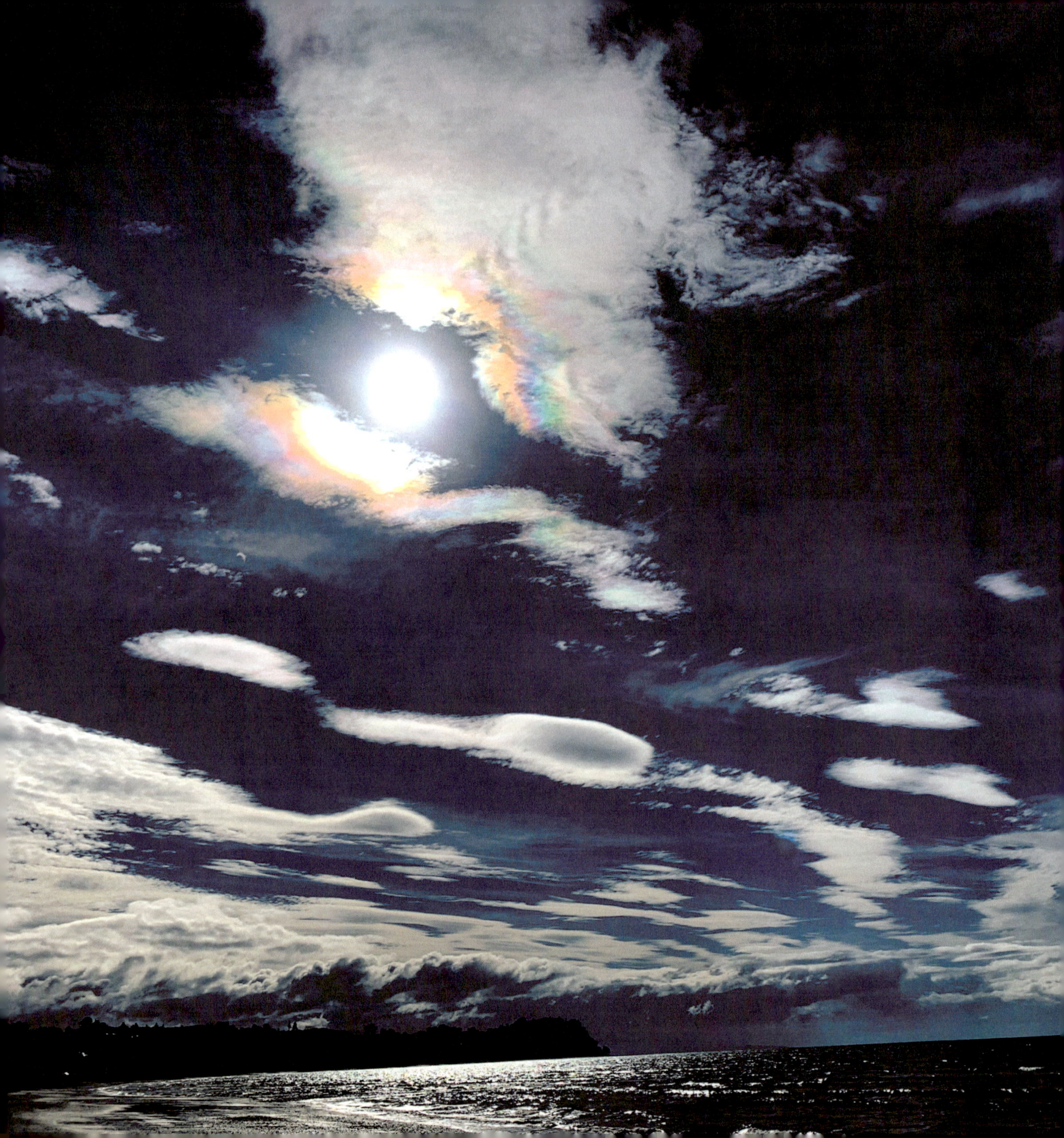

Bible verse:

Personal prayer:

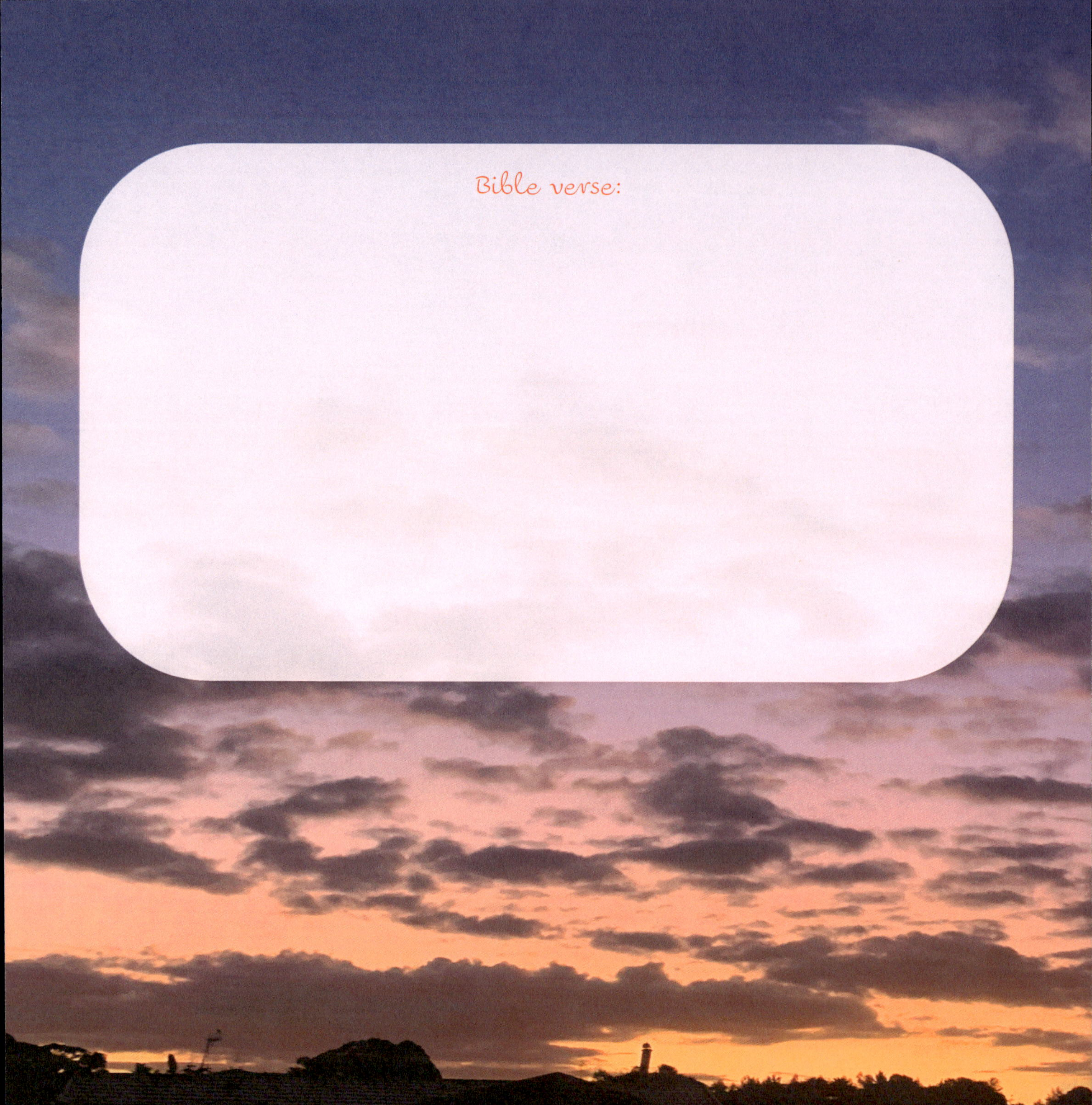
Bible verse:

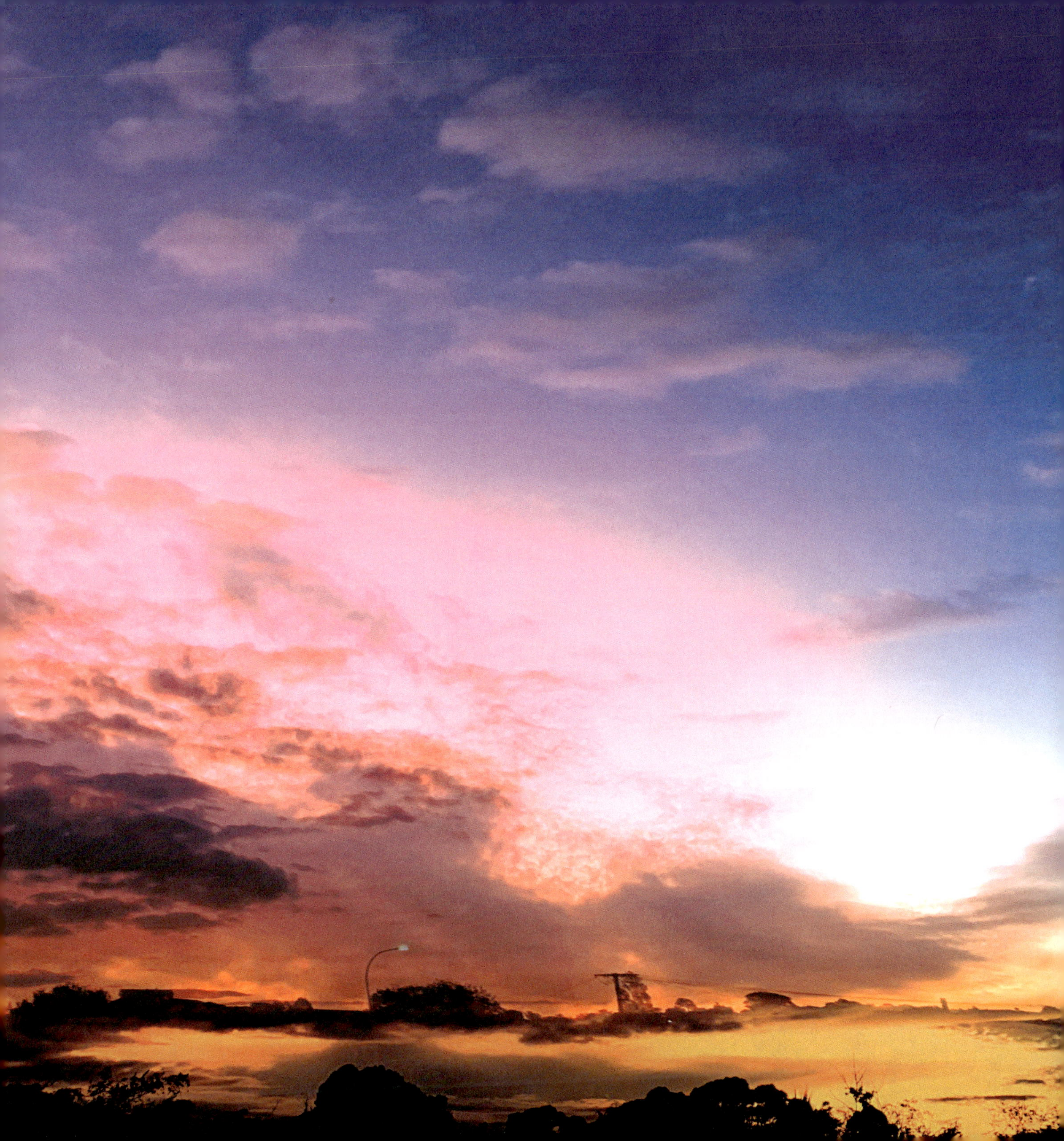

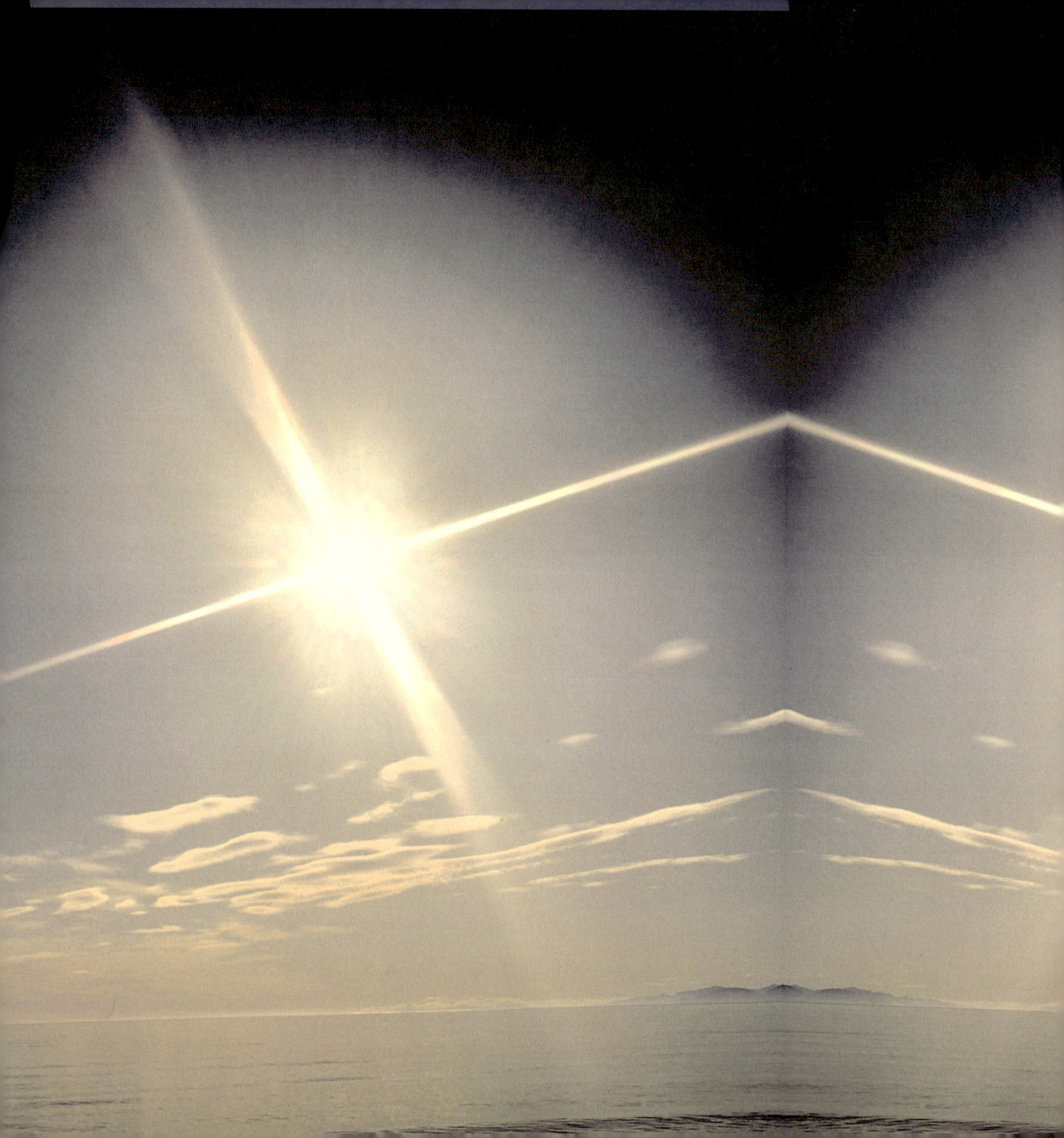

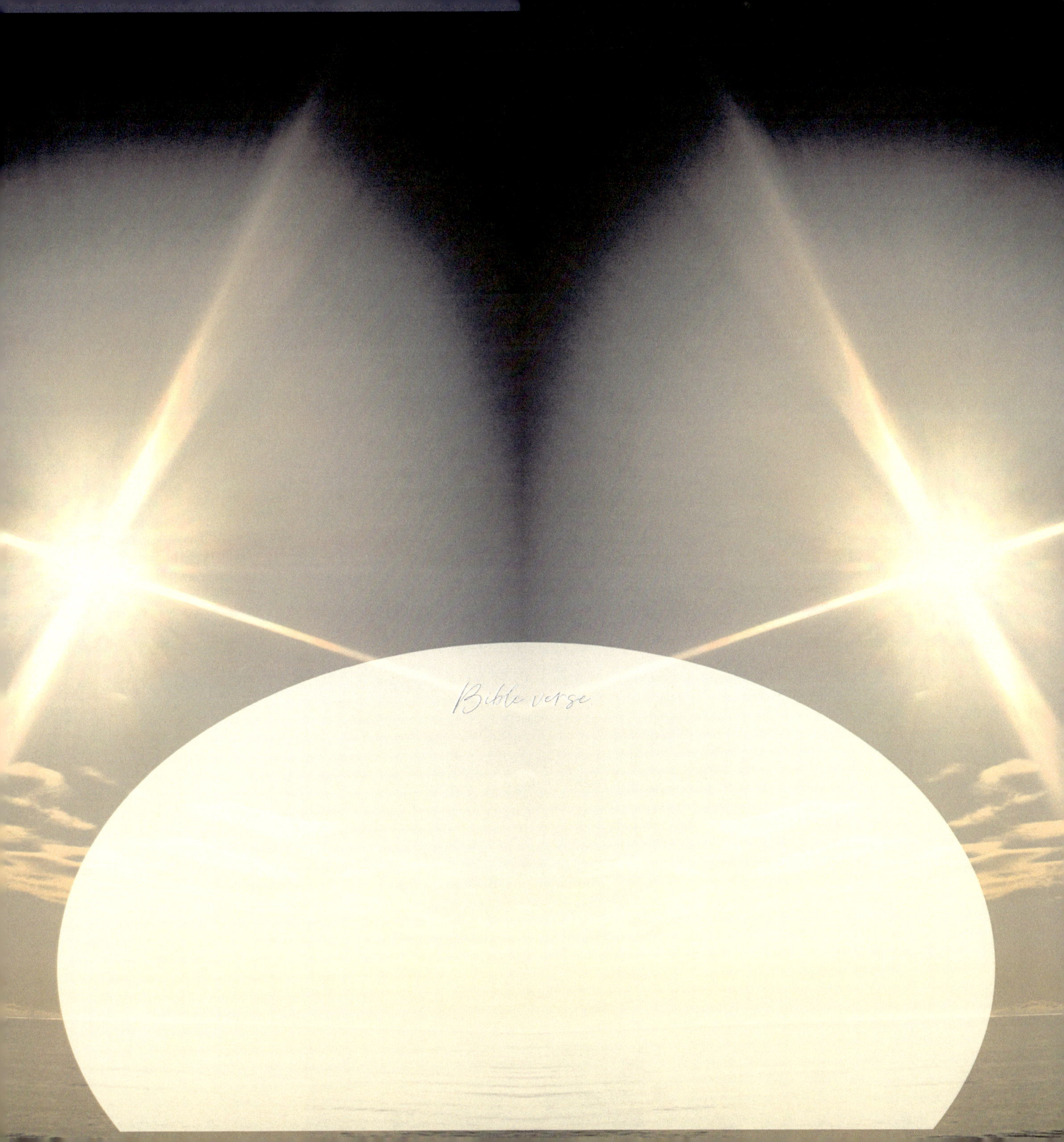
Bible verse

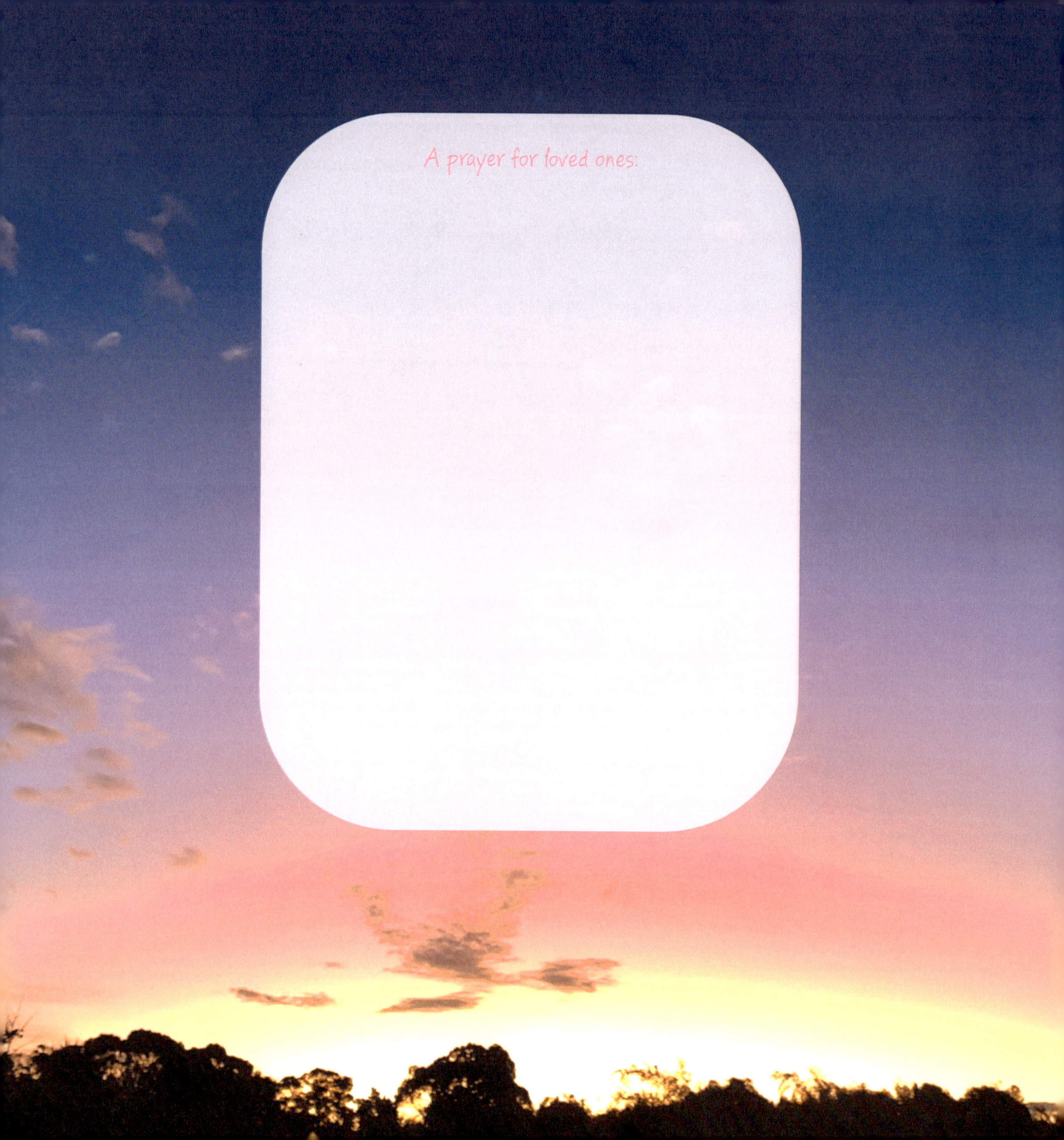

A prayer for loved ones:

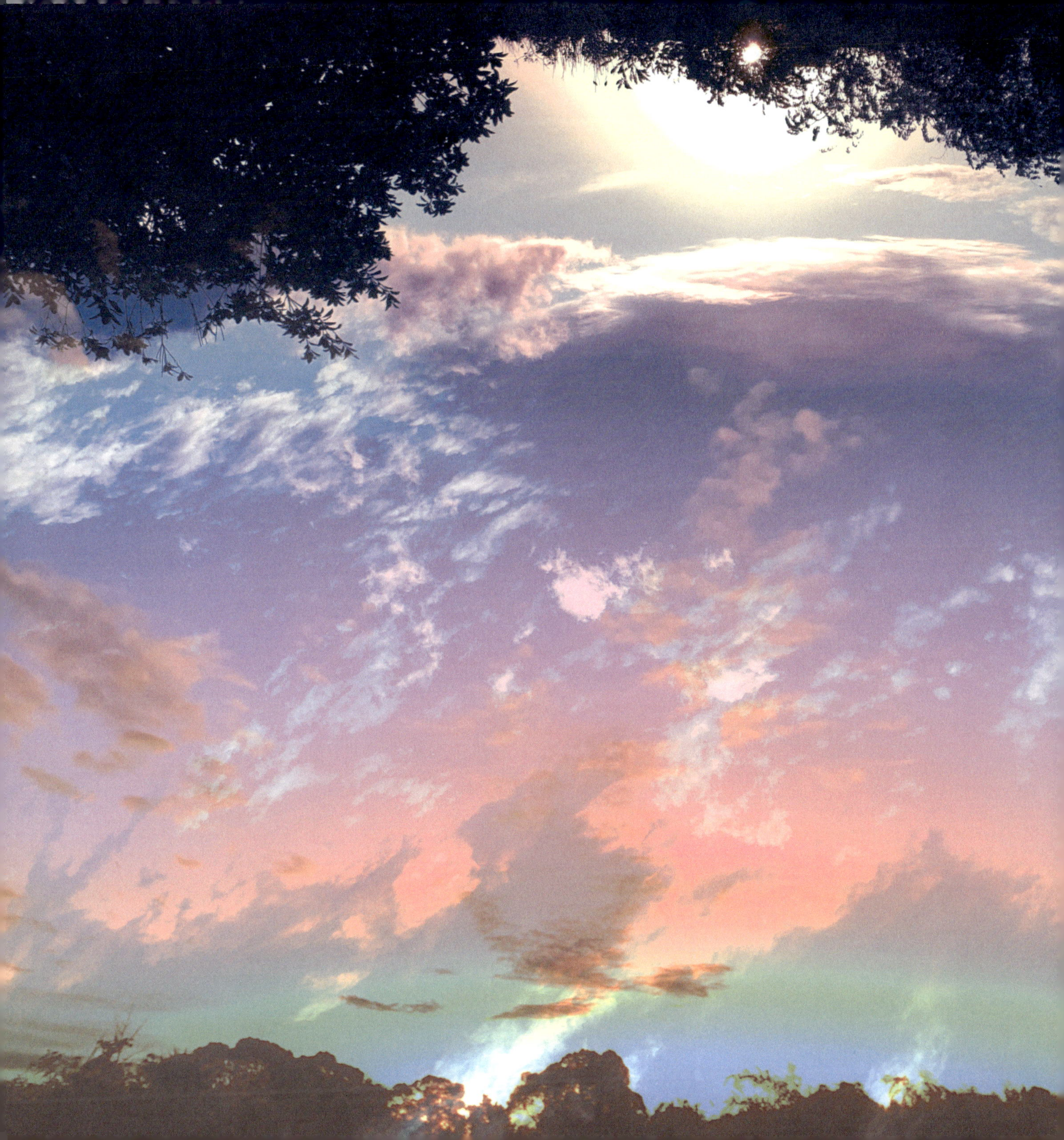

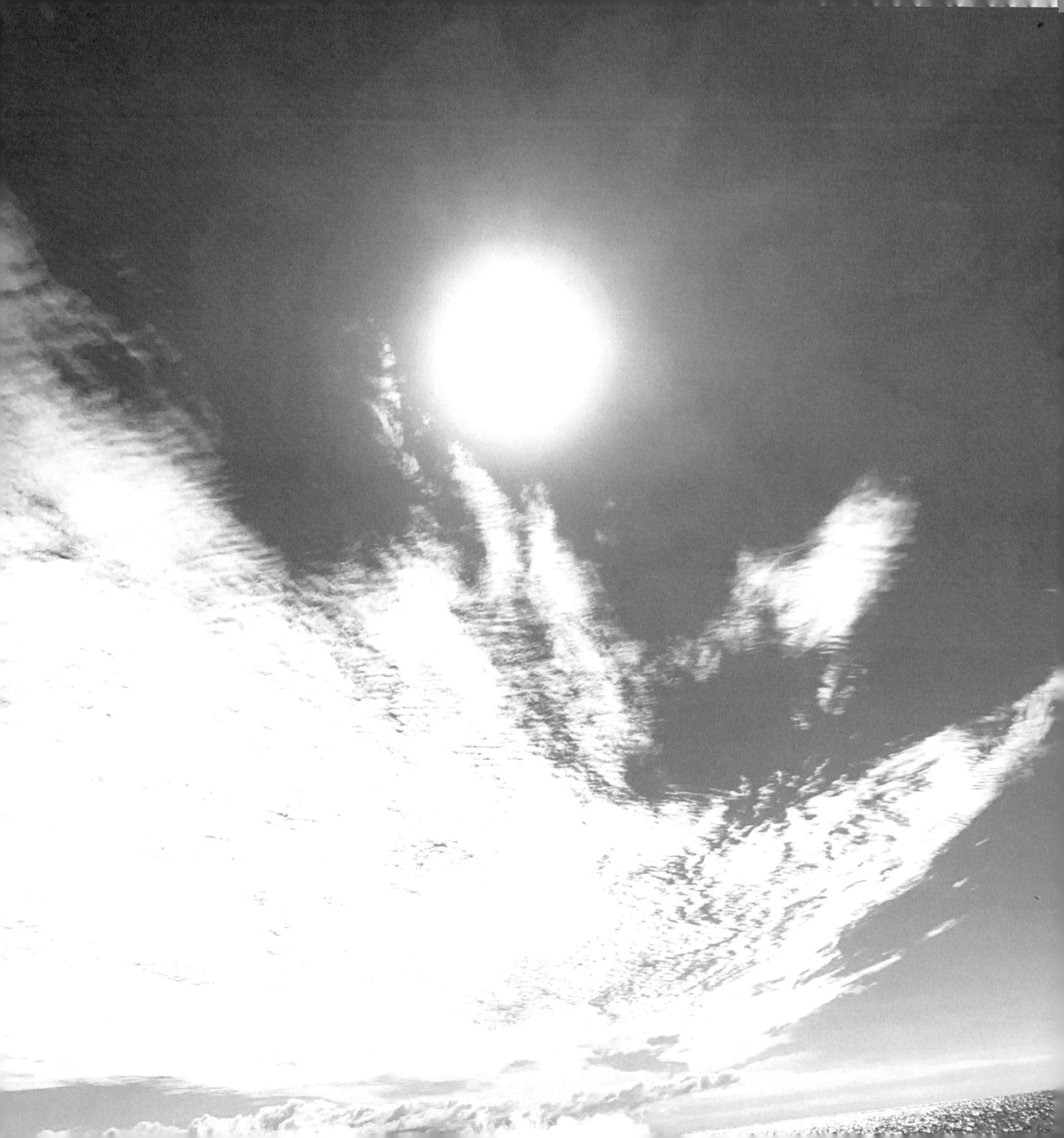

Bible verse:

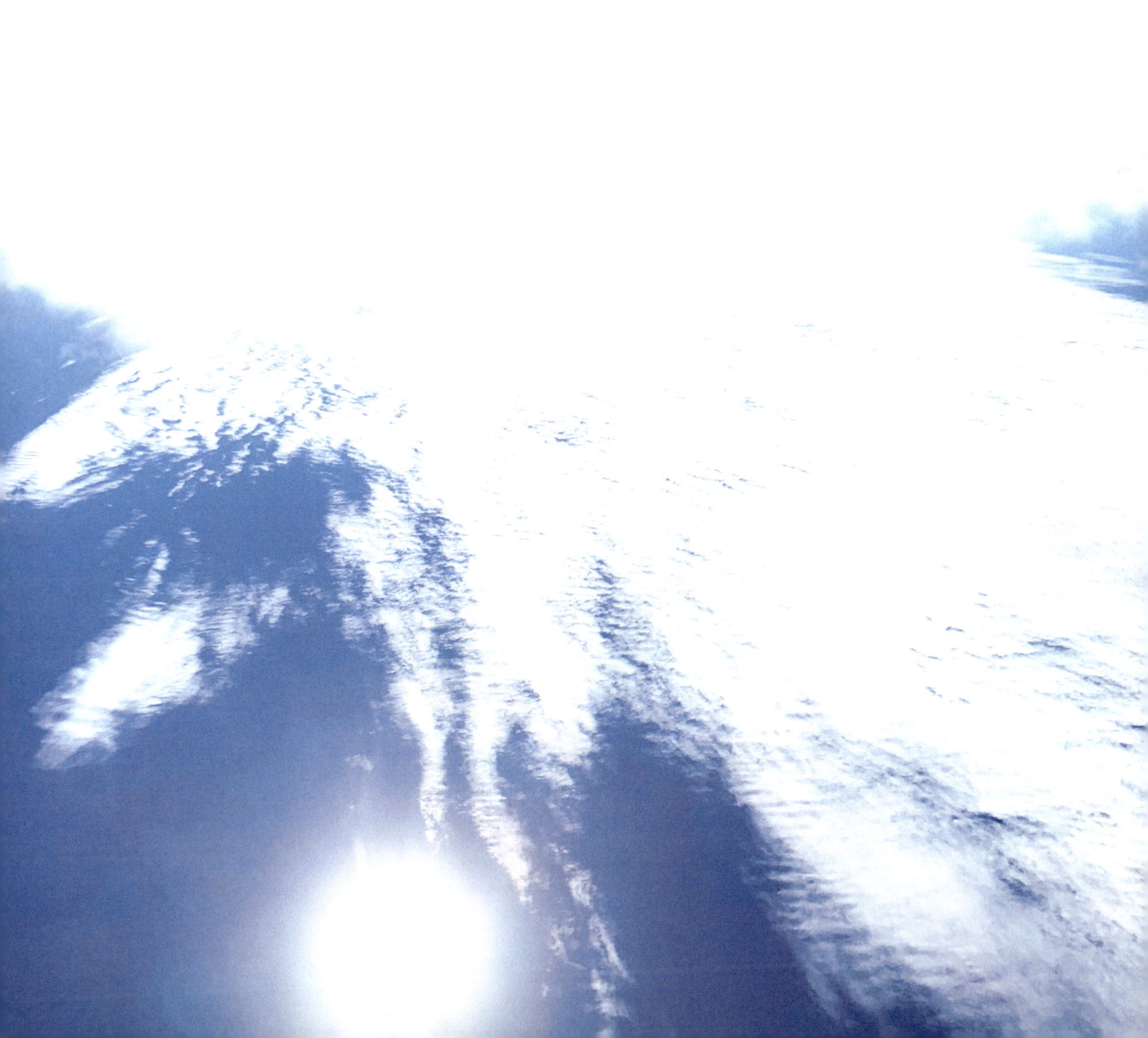

Bible verse:

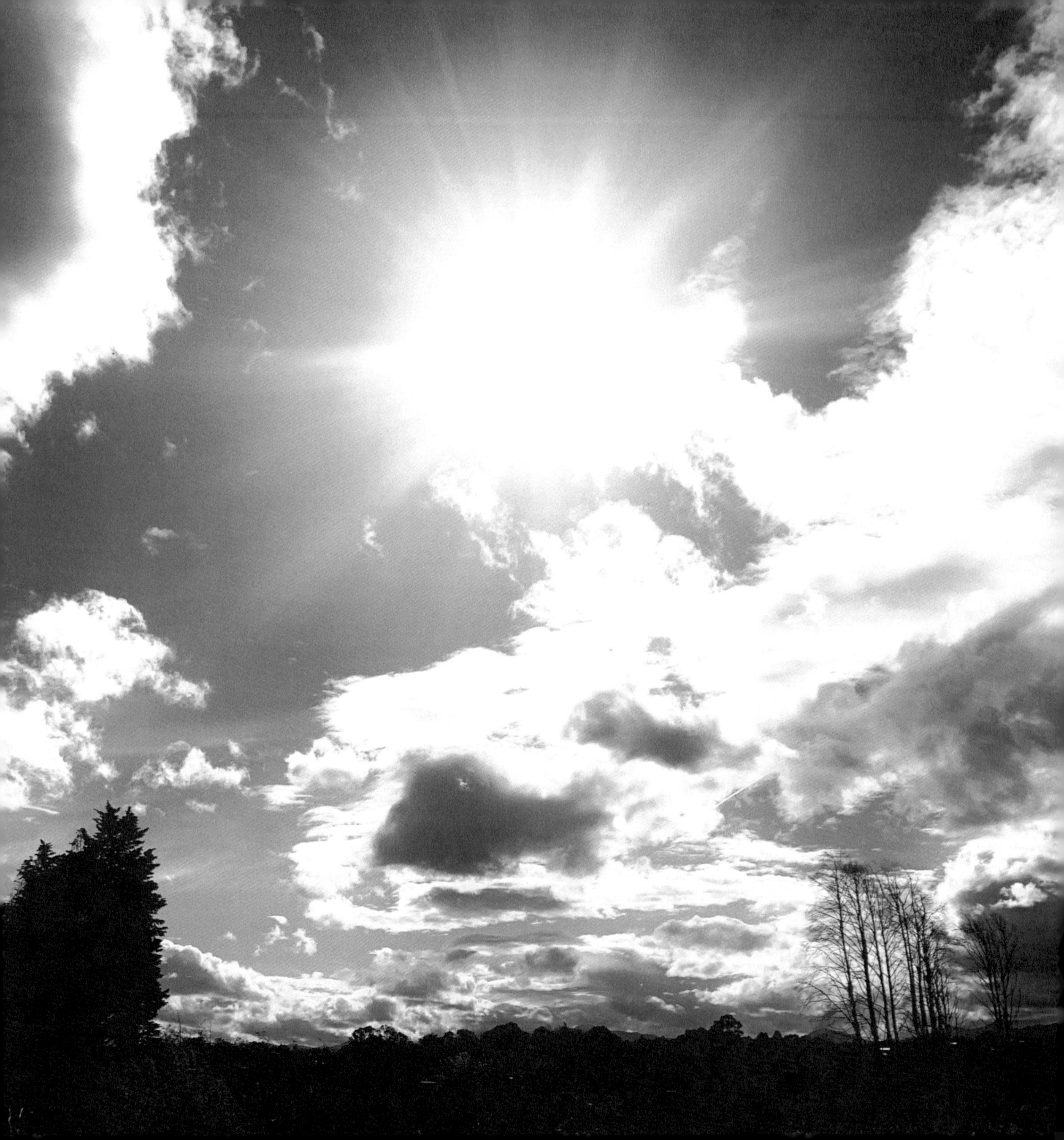

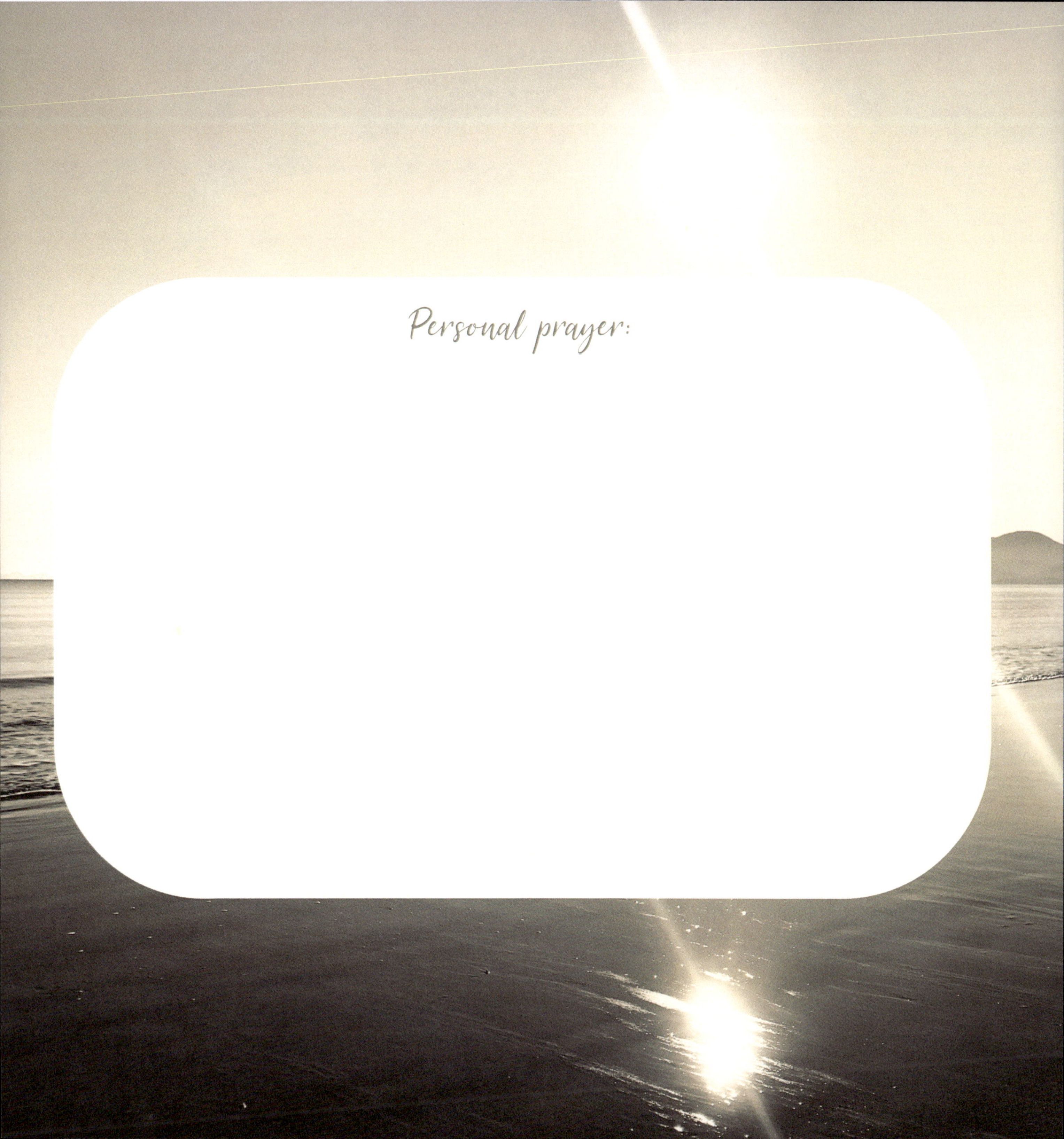
Personal prayer:

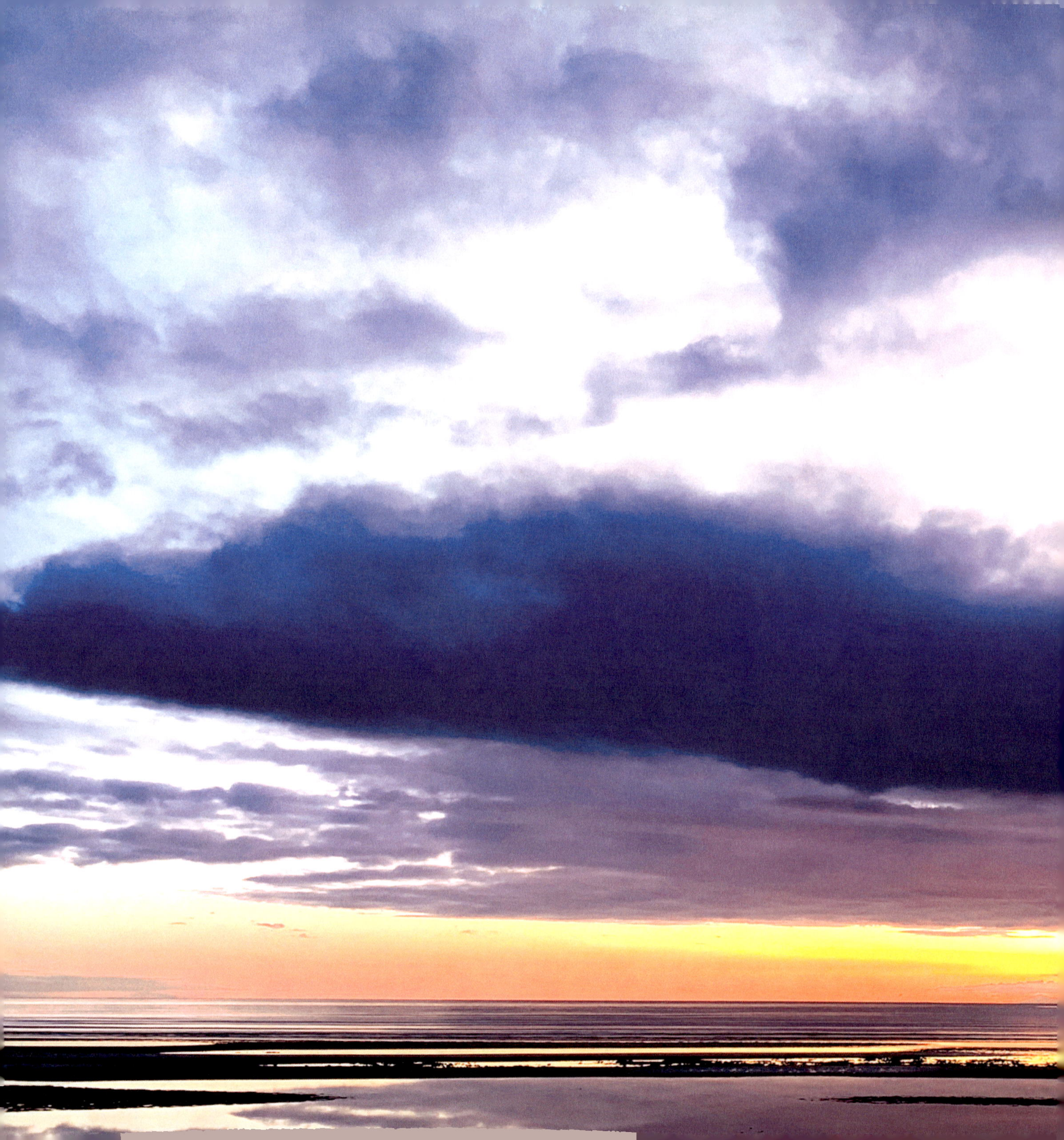

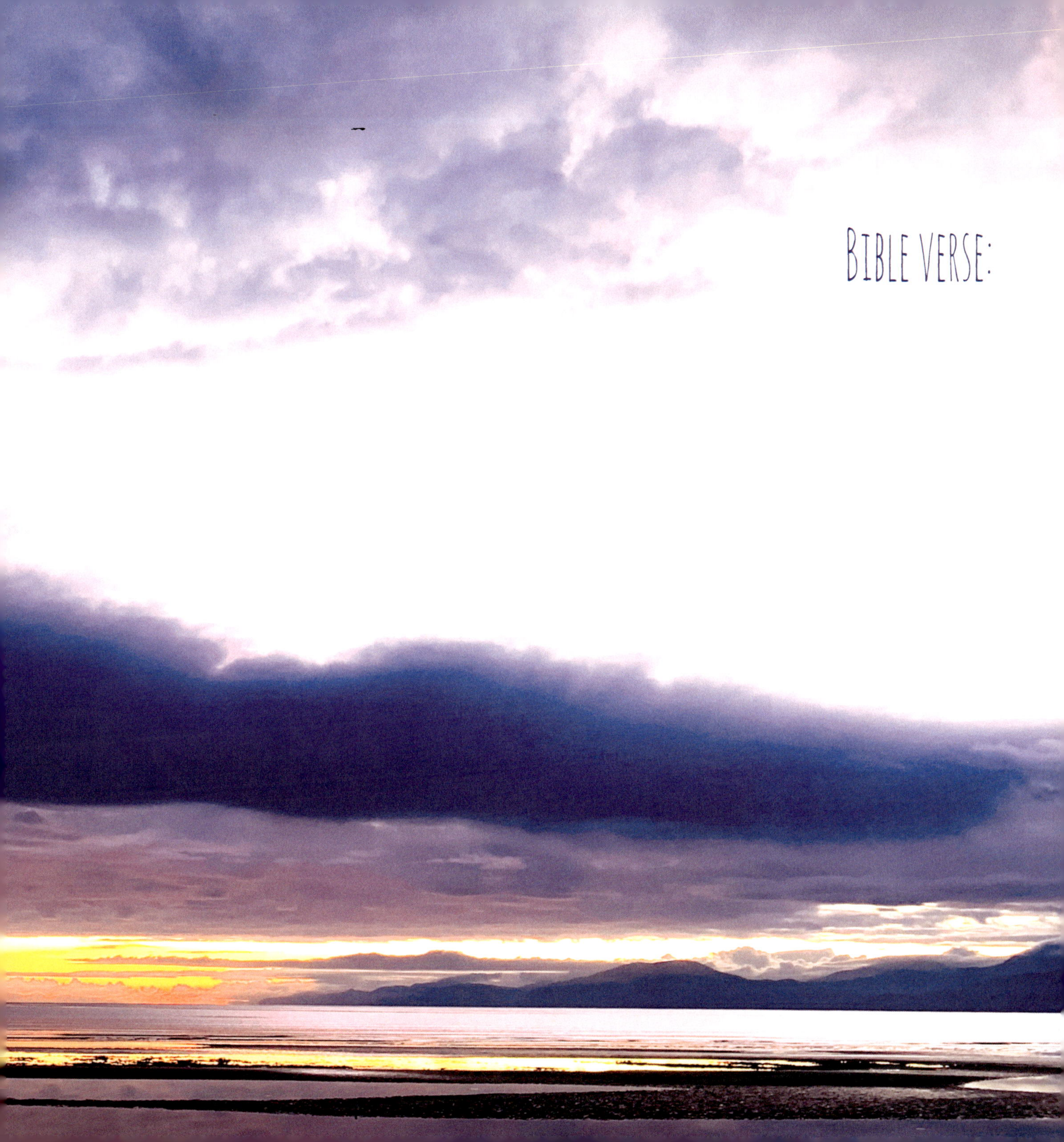

Bible verse:

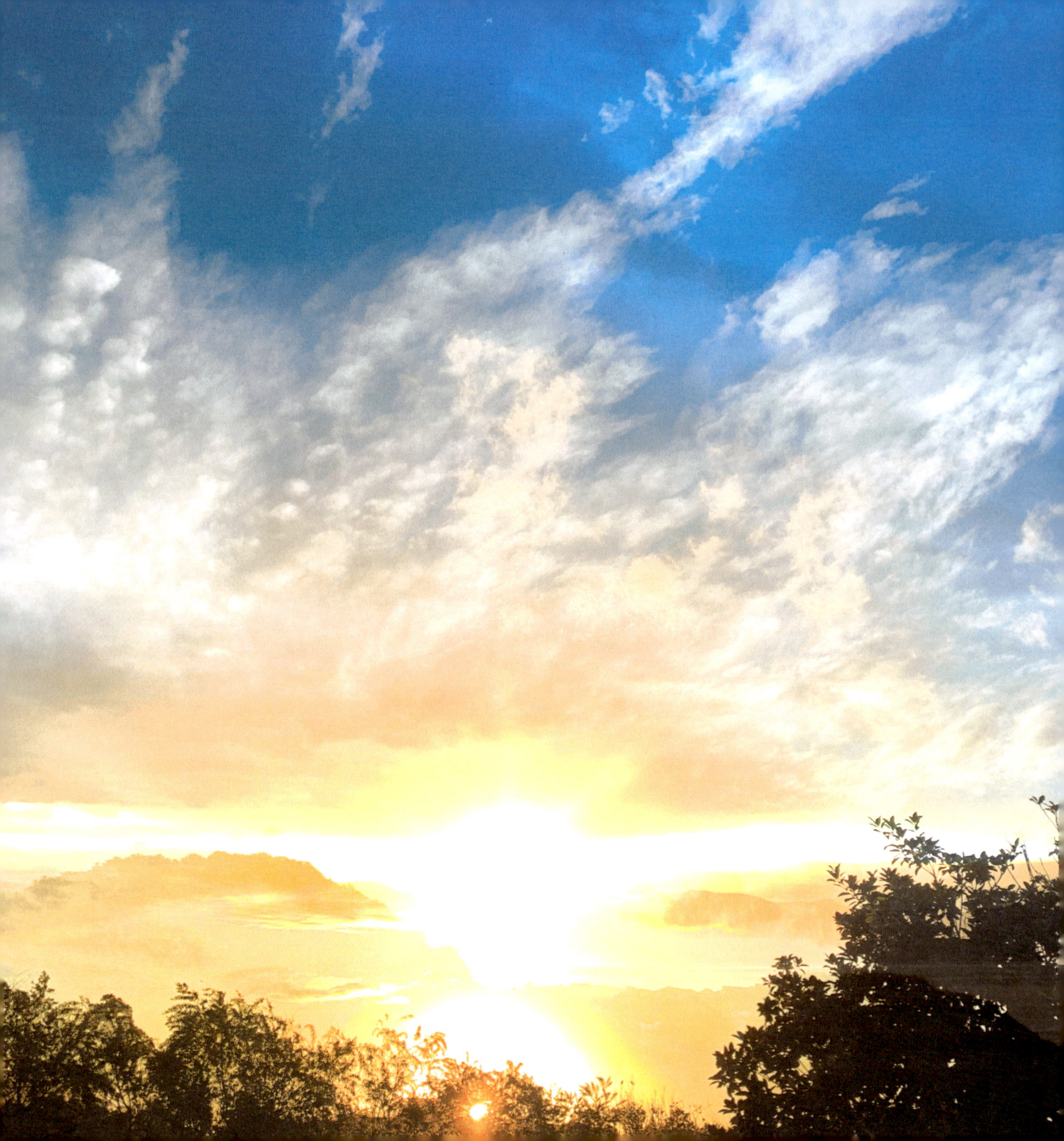

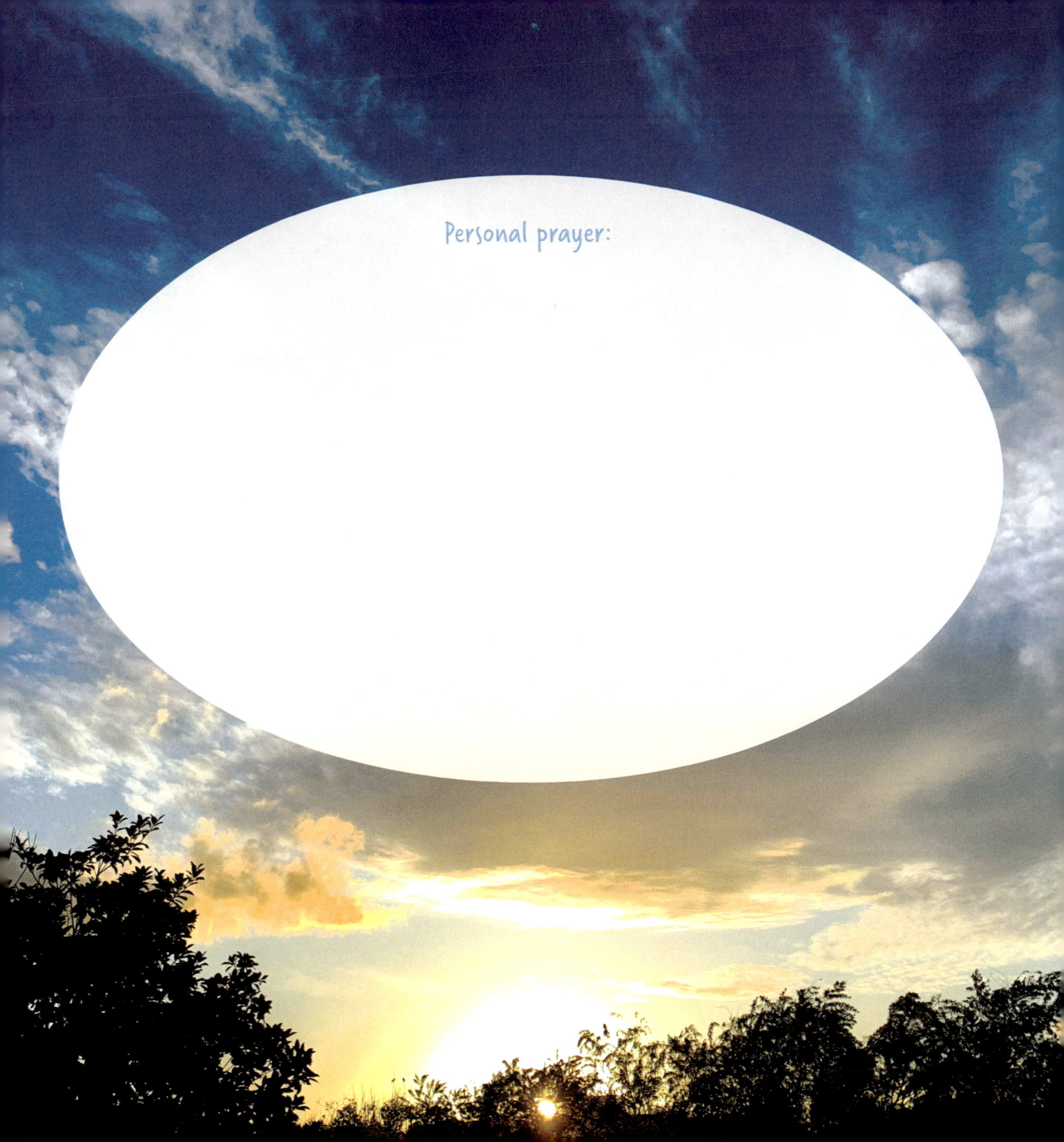
Personal prayer:

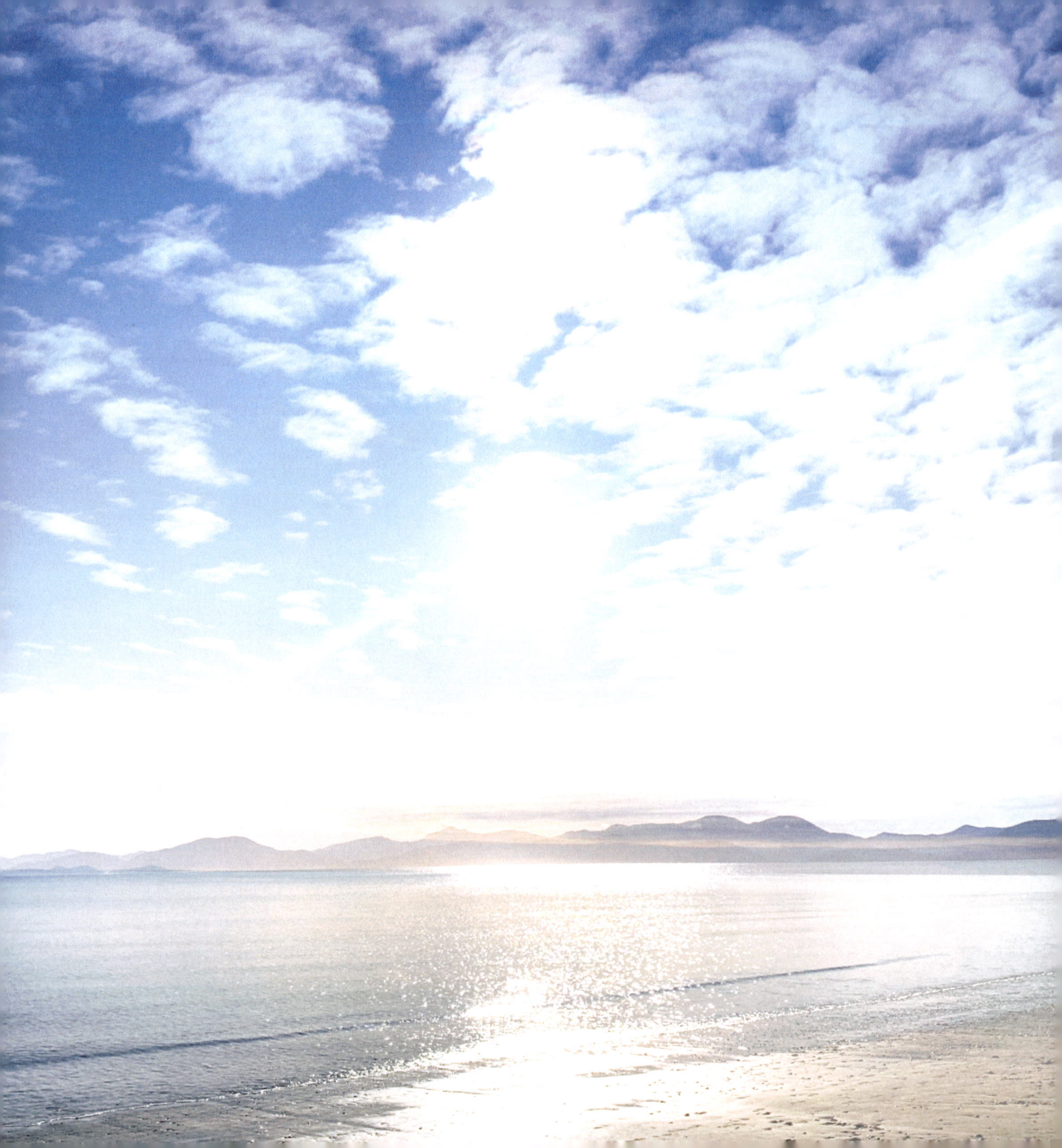

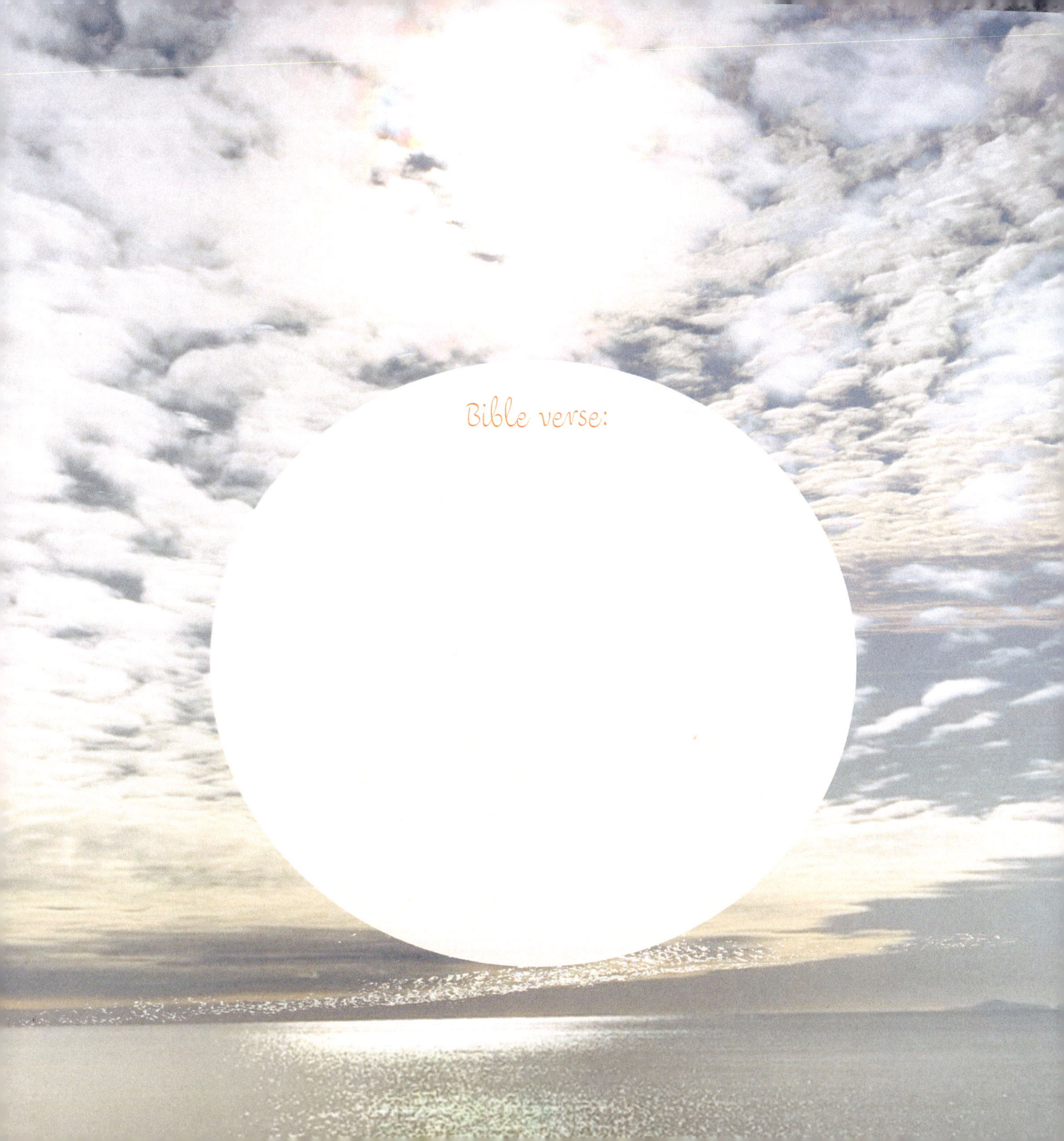
Bible verse:

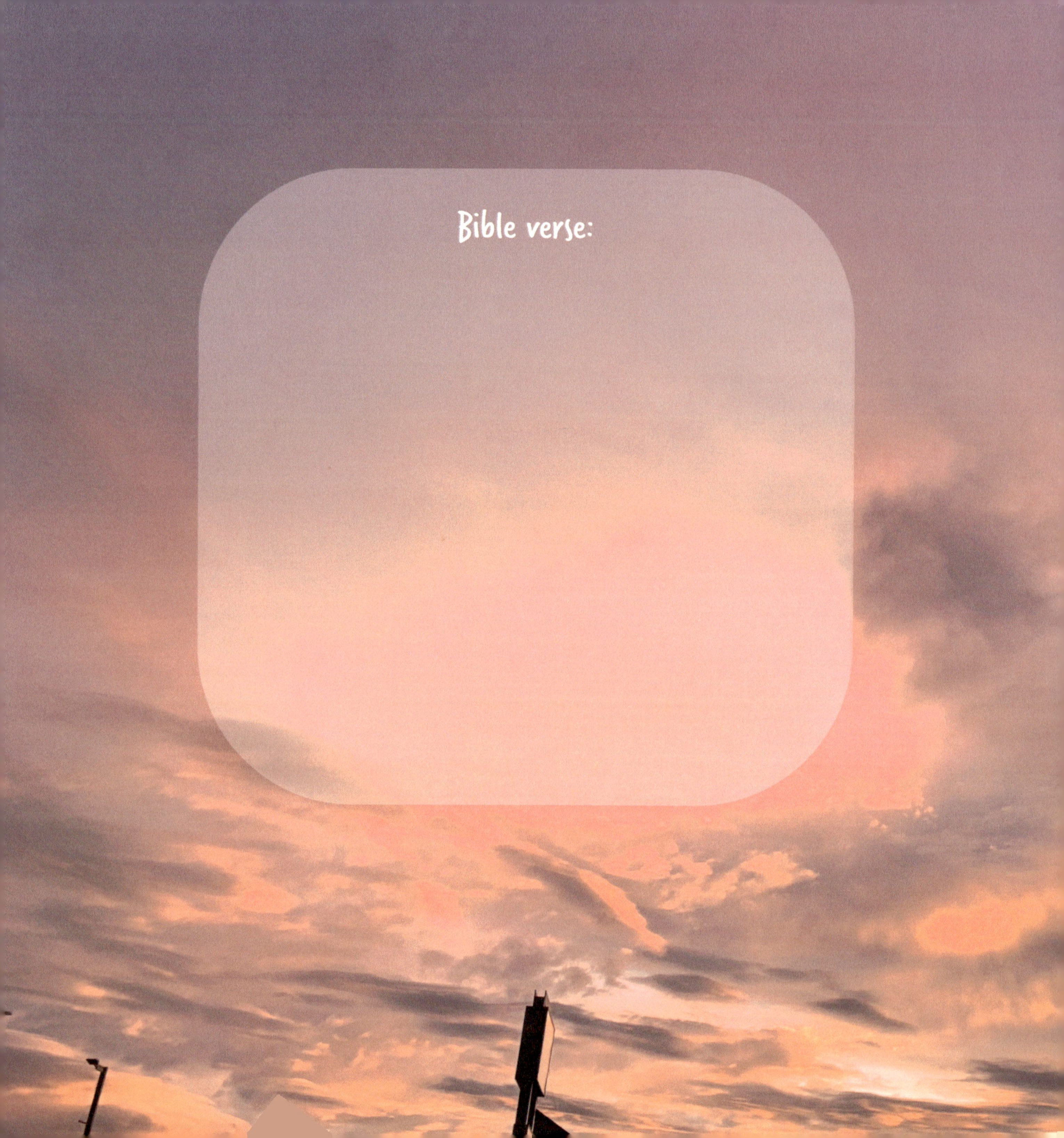
Bible verse:

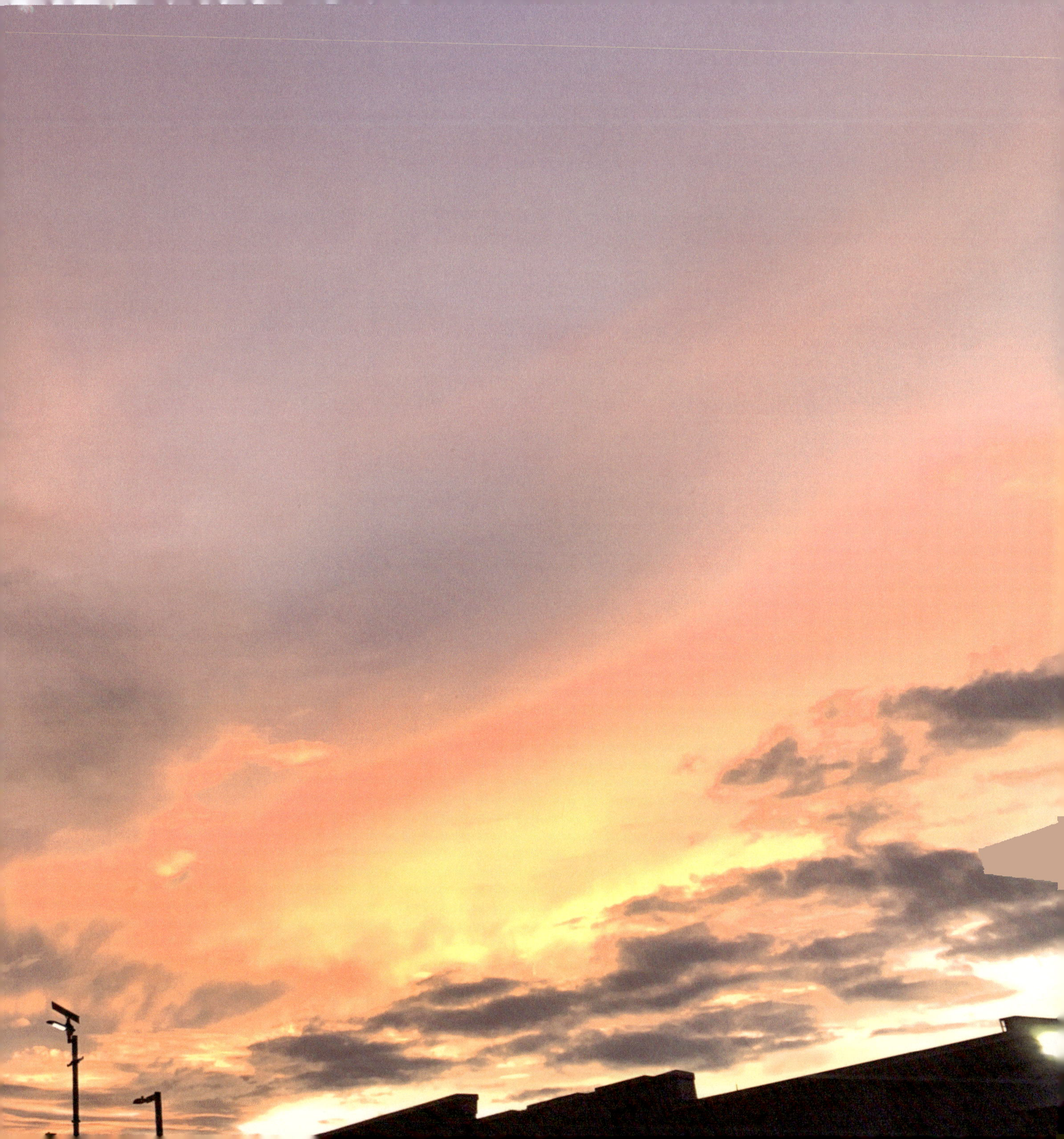

Bible verse:

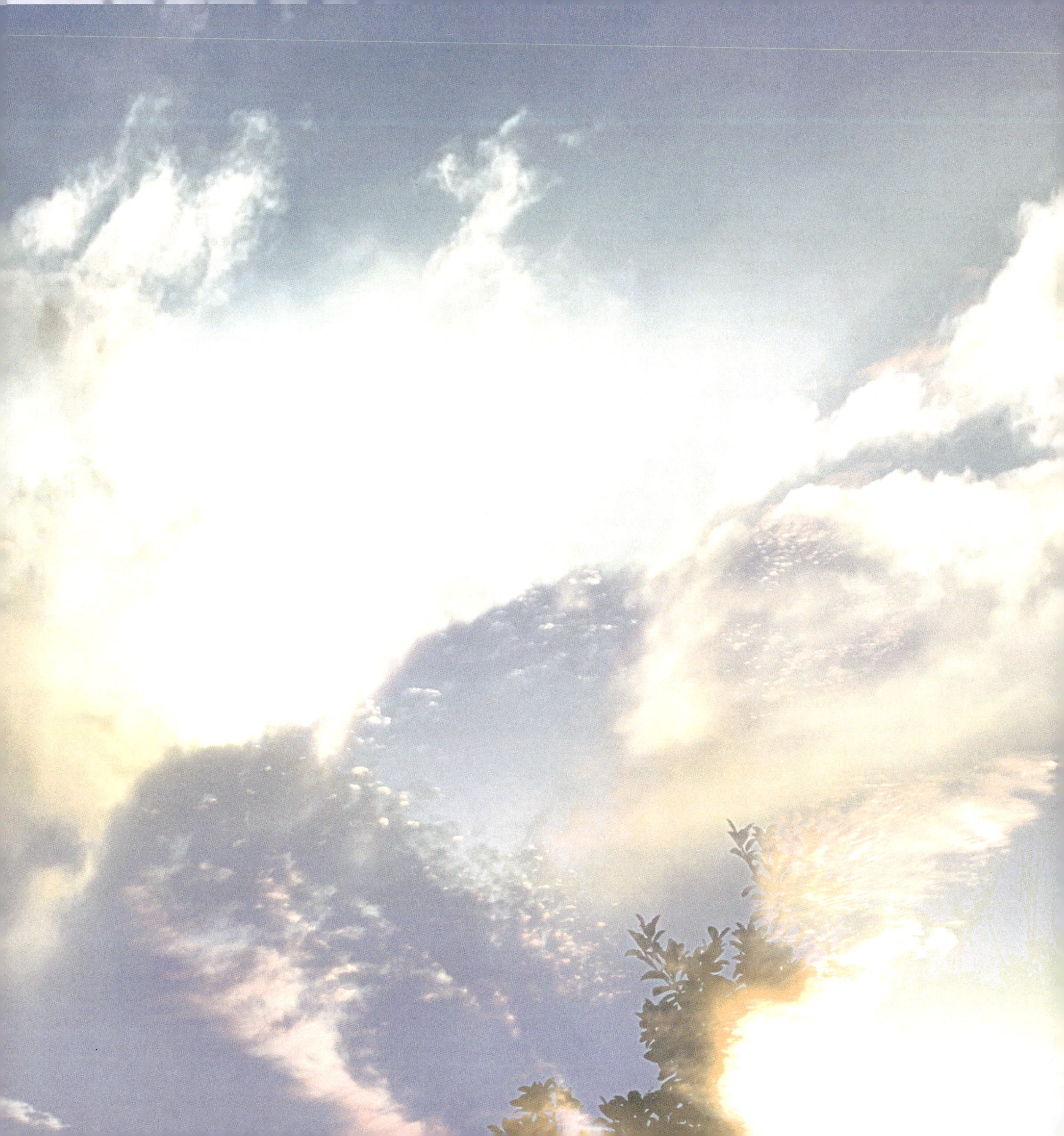

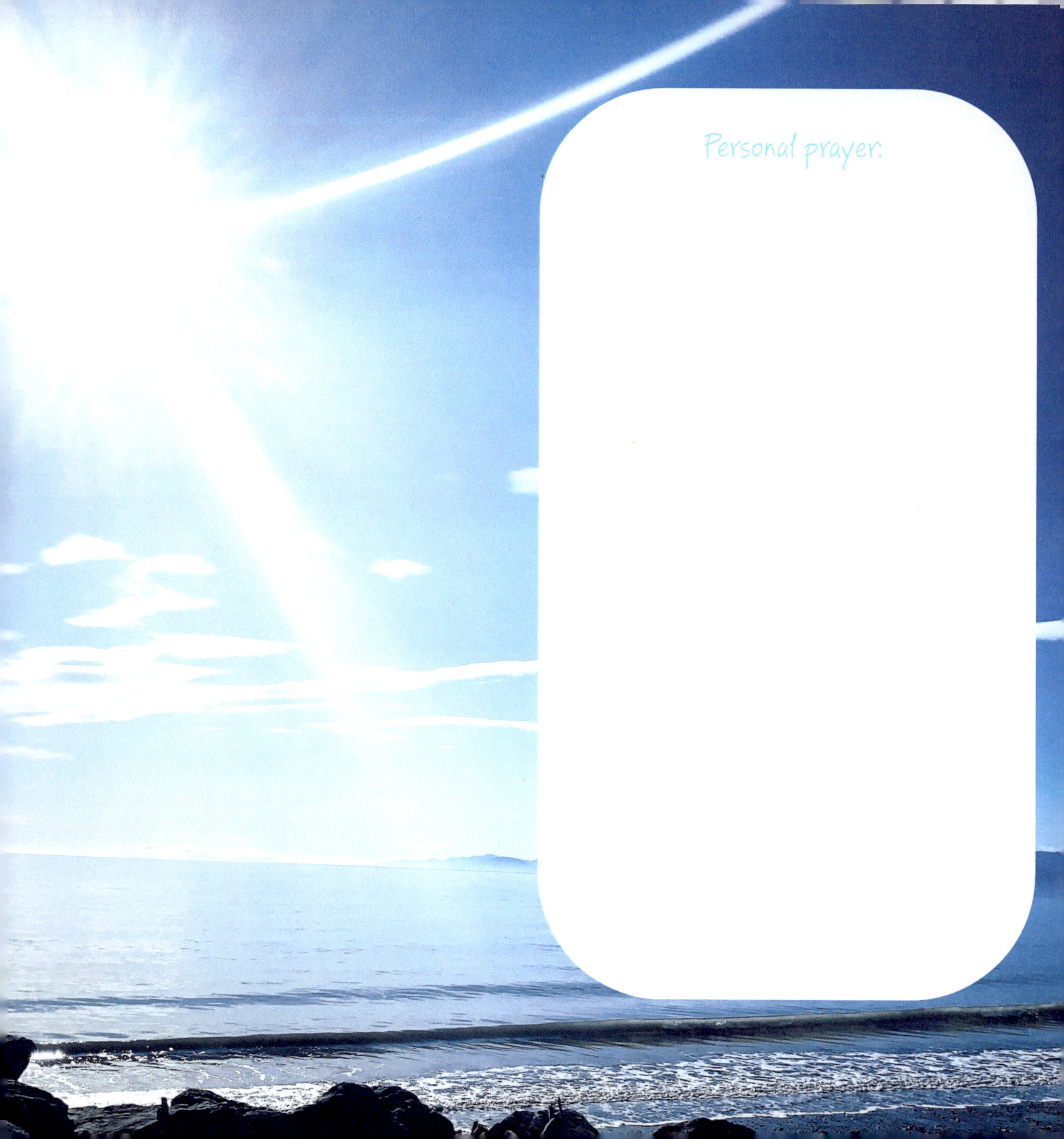
Personal prayer:

HEAVENWARD PRAYERS SCRIPTURE ART

Published in New Zealand in 2025 by Dawnlight Publishing

ISBN 978-1-99-117673-8 (hardcover)
ISBN 978-1-99-117672-1 (paperback)

Scripture Art Books

Scripture Art books with verses. Available in a coffee-table style hardcover edition and a smaller paperback gift size.

Writeable Scripture Art Books with space to write in your own Bible verses and prayers.

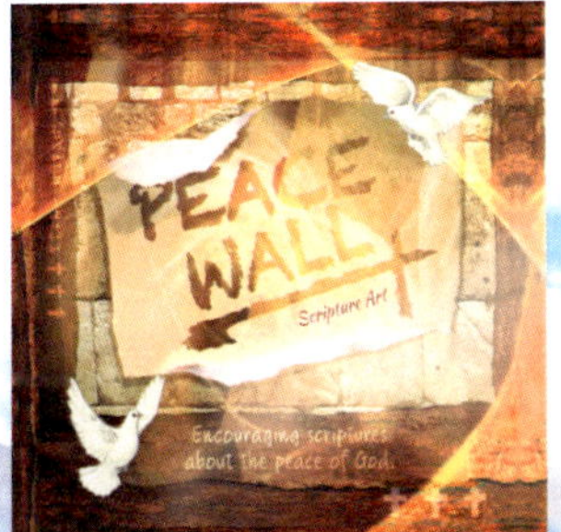

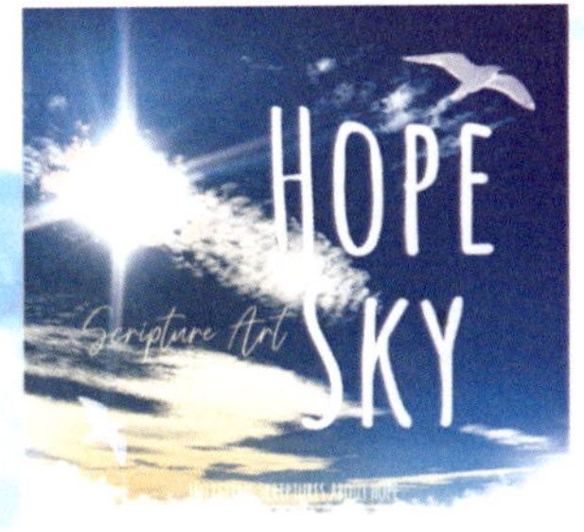

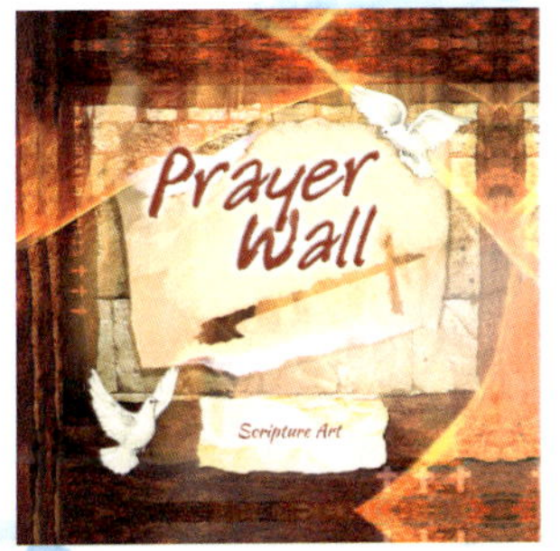

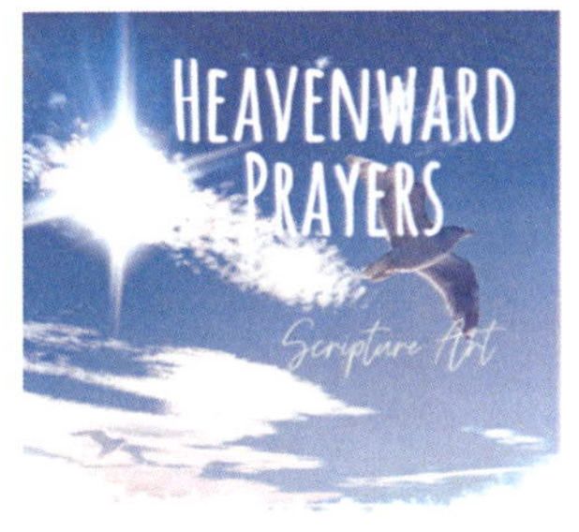